Alfred's Premier Piano Course

Dennis Alexander • Gayle Kowalchyk • E. L. Lancaster • Victoria McArthur • Martha Mier

Alfred's *Premier Piano Course* Christmas Book 6 includes familiar Christmas pieces that reinforce concepts included in Lesson Book 6. The music continues the strong pedagogical focus of the course while providing the enjoyment of playing familiar music during the Christmas season.

Christmas Book 6 is not correlated page-by-page with Lesson Book 6, but the pieces use only the concepts that are introduced in Lesson Book 6. They are arranged in progressive order of difficulty, with the easiest pieces first, though it is not necessary to progress straight through the book.

Allowing students to study music they enjoy during the Christmas season is highly motivating. Consequently, reading and rhythm skills often improve greatly when studying holiday music. The authors hope that the music in Christmas 6 brings hours of enjoyment to this festive season. Merry Christmas!

Edited by Morton Manus

Cover Design by Ted Engelbart
Interior Design by Tom Gerou
Illustrations by Jimmy Holder
Music Engraving by Linda Lusk

CONTENTS

Produced by
Alfred Music Publishing Co., Inc.
P.O. Box 10003
Van Nuys, CA 91410-0003
alfred.com

Printed in USA.

ISBN-10: 0-7390-7554-3
ISBN-13: 978-0-7390-7554-8

In 1818, just before Christmas, Father Joseph Mohr noticed that his church organ was damaged and unplayable. He needed something to sing on Christmas Eve, so he quickly wrote some lyrics and gave them to his organist, Franz Grüber. Mohr asked Grüber to compose a simple melody that could be accompanied by a few guitar chords. ***Silent Night*** *was the result of their collaboration and has been translated into over 44 languages.*

Silent Night

Franz Grüber

17
21
25
rit.
29
a tempo
LH over
34
LH over
poco rit.

Have Yourself a Merry Little Christmas *was originally sung in the 1944 movie* Meet Me in St. Louis. *Its story is about an average American family that goes to the 1904 World's Fair. The movie's score is full of great songs, and* Have Yourself a Merry Little Christmas *is one of them. It was sung in the film by Judy Garland and became an all-time favorite Christmas classic.*

Have Yourself a Merry Little Christmas

Words and Music by
Hugh Martin and Ralph Blane

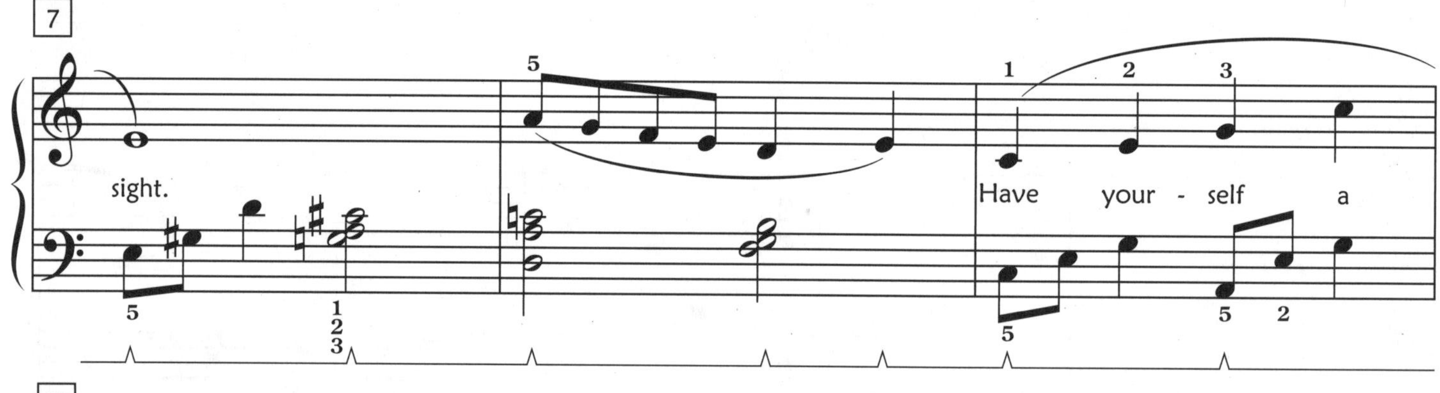

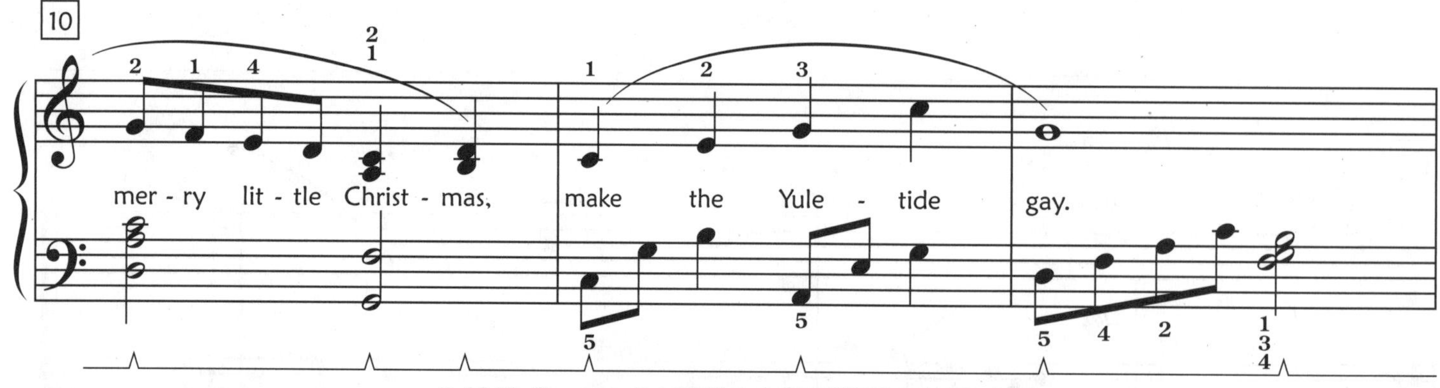

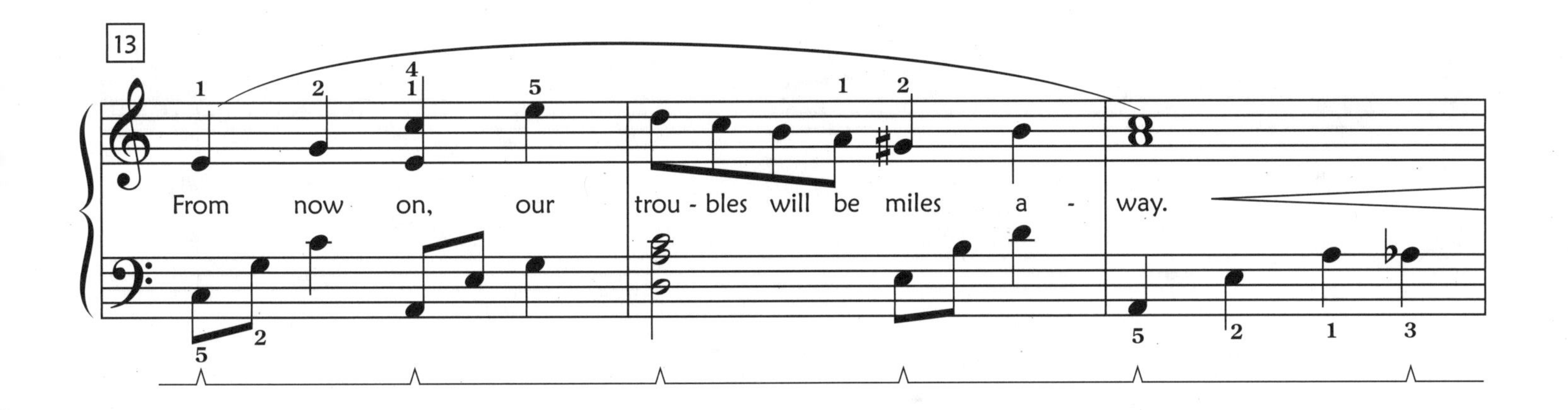
13
From now on, our trou - bles will be miles a - way.

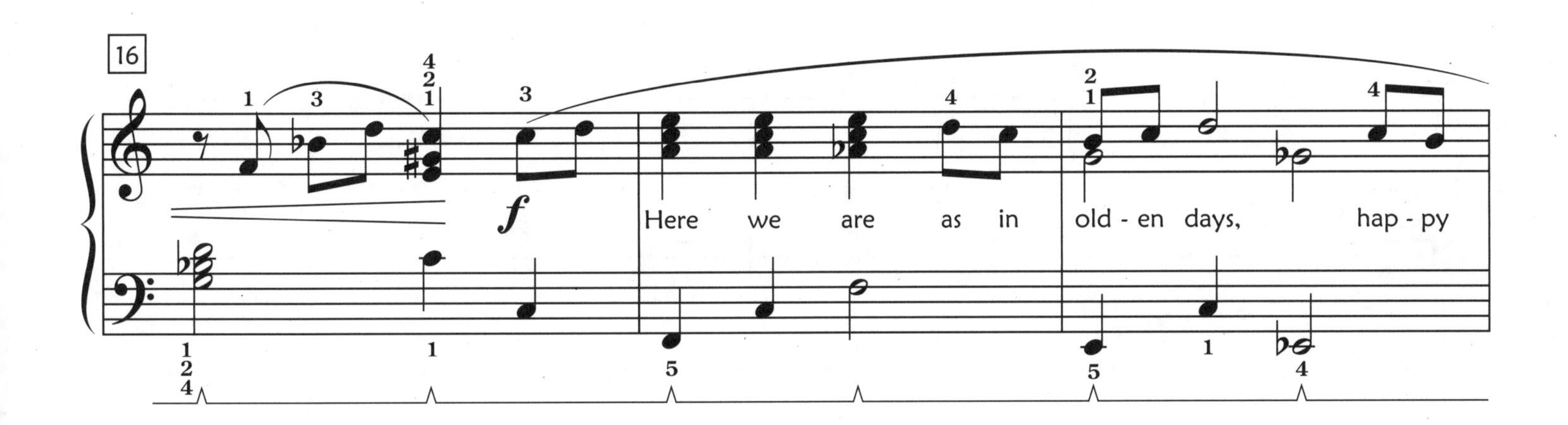
16
f
Here we are as in old - en days, hap - py

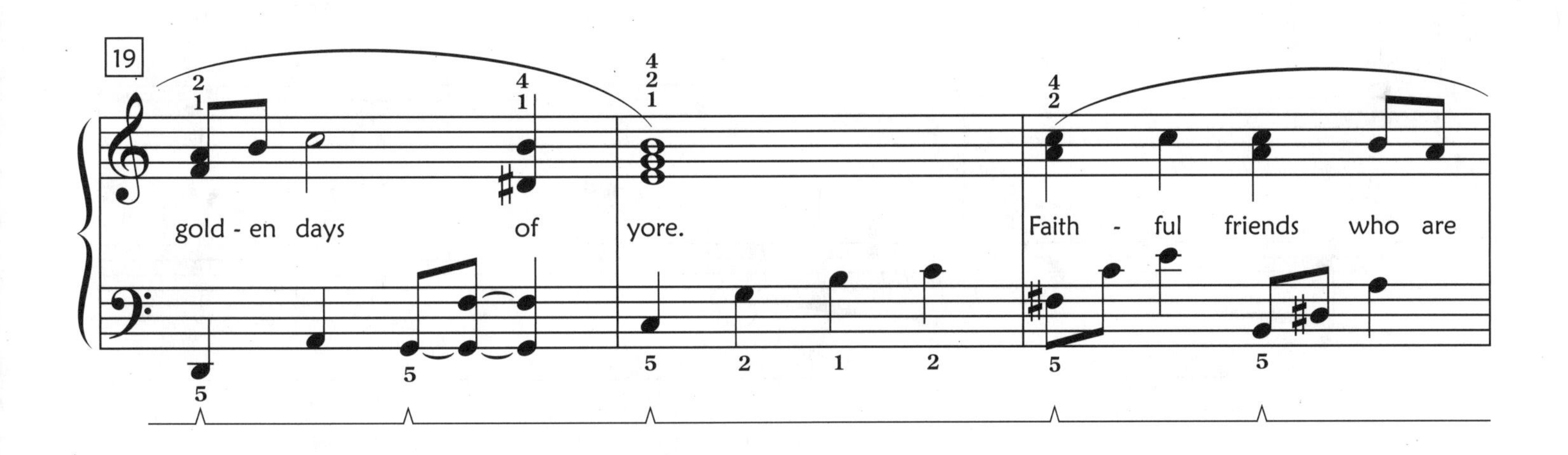
19
gold - en days of yore. Faith - ful friends who are

22
dear to us gath - er near to us once more.

25
mf
Through the years we all will be to - geth - er, if the fates al -
28
low. Hang a shin - ing star up - on the high - est
31
f
bough, and have your - self a
34
mer - ry lit - tle Christ - mas now.
rit.
mf
mp
pp

Lo, How a Rose E'er Blooming

Lo, How a Rose E'er Blooming *has been sung in Germany since the 16th century. In 1609, composer Michael Praetorius (1571–1621) harmonized the melody heard today. English words were added in 1894 by Theodore Baker. This carol is often sung as a haunting unaccompanied choral arrangement.*

Music by Michael Praetorius

13
p
16
mf
19
22
f
mp
25
LH
f

28
mp
f
31
mp
35
mf
38
p
41
rit.
pp

In the late 1830s in England, groups of carolers, called waits, would stroll through the streets of London, singing for a bit of pudding or a cup of good cheer. ***We Wish You a Merry Christmas*** *was originally a "waits' carol" and became very popular in the mid-19th century.*

We Wish You a Merry Christmas

Traditional English Carol

hap - py New Year!
mp
Broadly
f
poco rit.
Tempo I
mp
mf
mf
f

Leroy Anderson (1908–1975) was one of the finest composers of light music in the 20th century. His best-known works are The Syncopated Clock, Blue Tango, *and, of course,* **Sleigh Ride.** *It was said that Anderson got the idea for the piece during a heat wave in 1946. As proof of its popularity,* Sleigh Ride *has been performed and recorded by more musical artists than any other song in Western music.*

Sleigh Ride

Music by Leroy Anderson
Words by Mitchell Parish

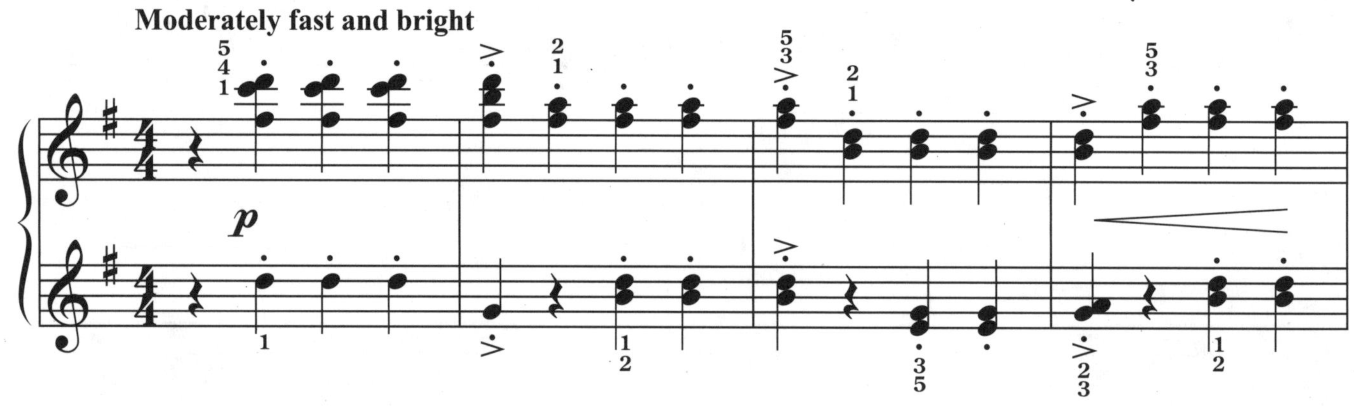

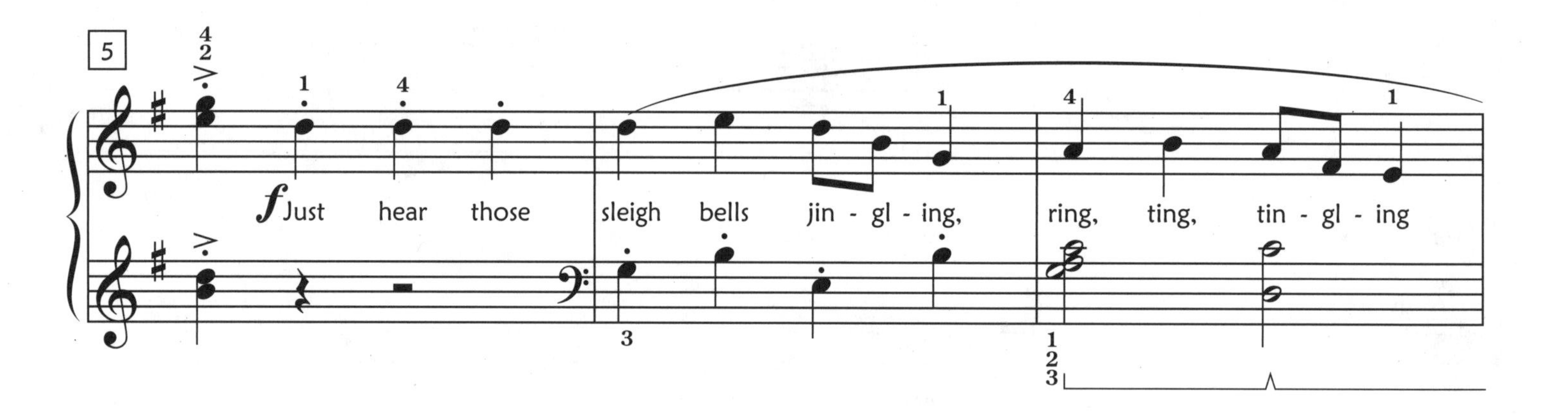

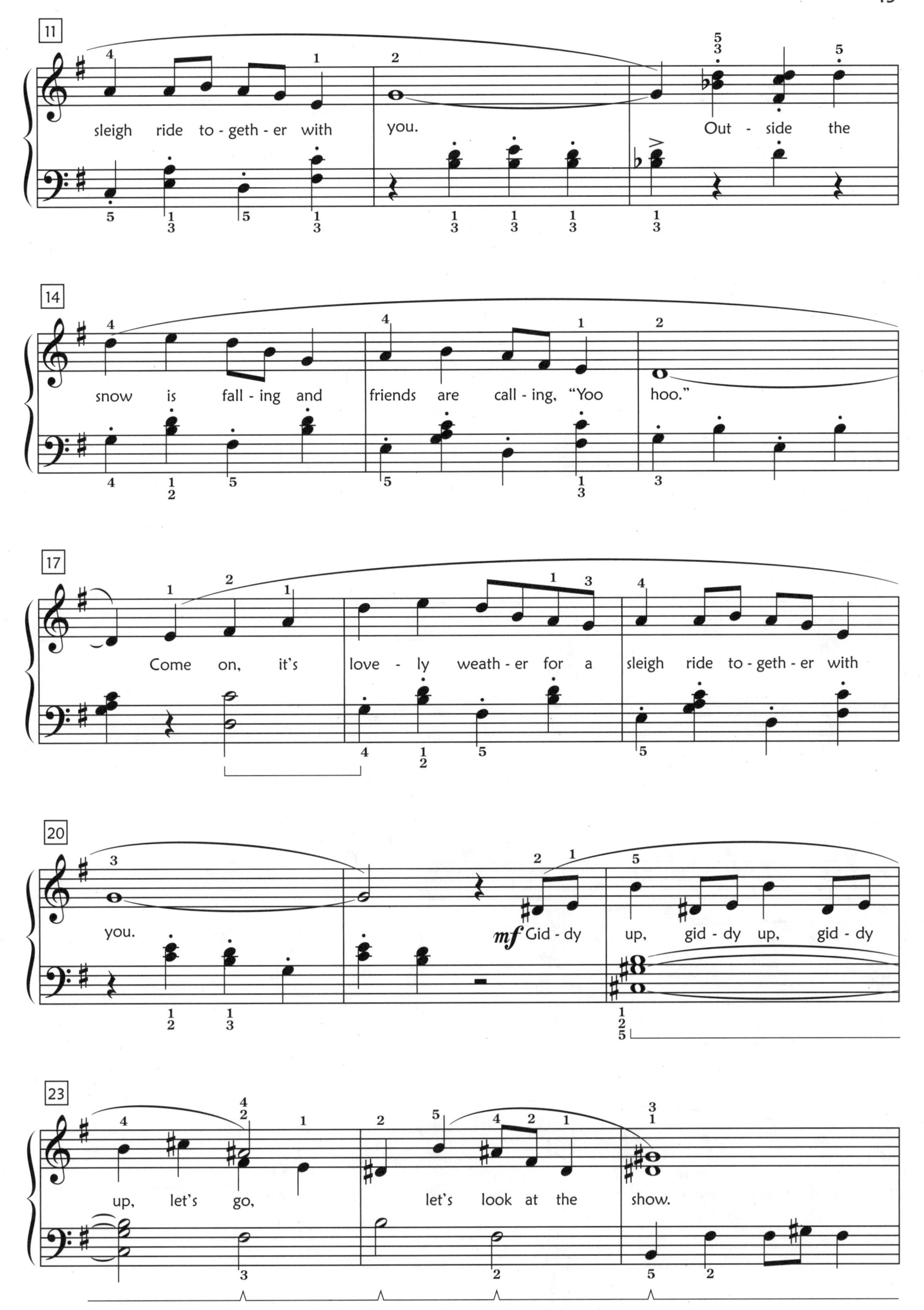
11
sleigh ride to - geth - er with
you.
Out - side the
14
snow is fall - ing and
friends are call - ing, "Yoo
hoo."
17
Come on, it's
love - ly weath - er for a
sleigh ride to - geth - er with
20
you.
mf Gid - dy
up, gid - dy up, gid - dy
23
up, let's go,
let's look at the
show.

26
We're riding in a wonder-land of snow.
29
Giddy up, giddy up, giddy up, it's grand,
32
just holding your hand.
We're gliding a-
35
long with a song of a winter-y fair-y land. Our cheeks are
f
38
nice and ros-y and comfy cozy are we.

We're snug - gled up to - geth - er like two birds of a feath - er would
be. Let's take that road be - fore us and
sing a cho - rus or two. Come on, it's
love - ly weath - er for a sleigh ride to - geth - er with you.
mp

Originally called **Deck the Hall** (with no s), this Welsh melody is from the 16th century. The original Welsh words were about New Year's night; the familiar words printed here date from the 1880s. In many versions the "fa la la" is played by a harp. Even today, the holly's red berries and green leaves mentioned in the carol are traditional colors of the holiday.

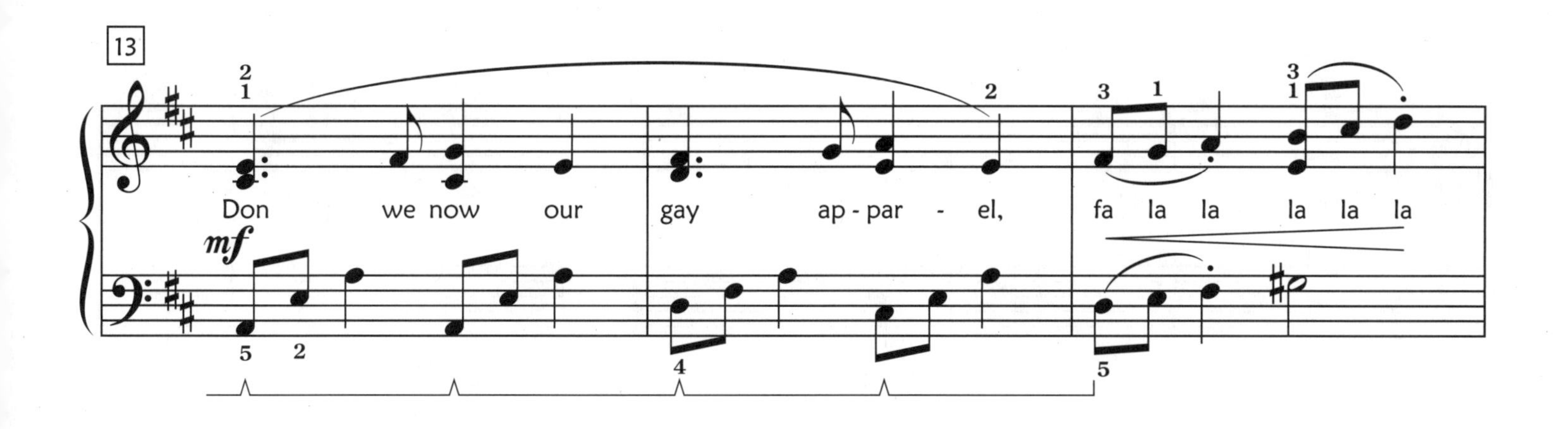
13
Don we now our gay ap - par - el, fa la la la la la
mf

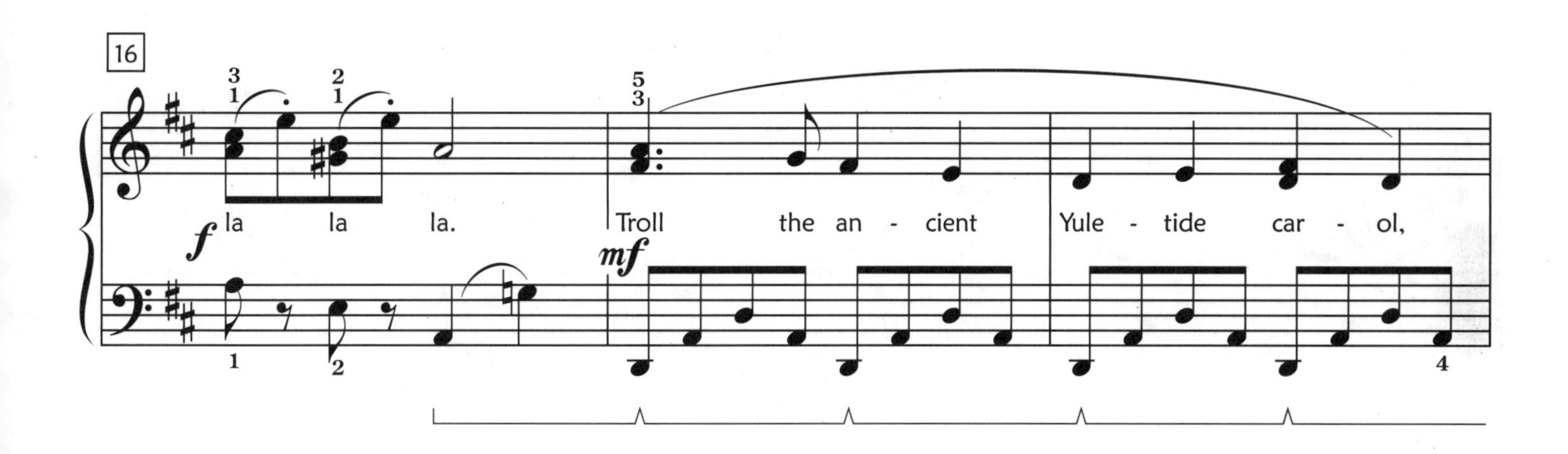
16
la la la. Troll the an - cient Yule - tide car - ol,
f
mf

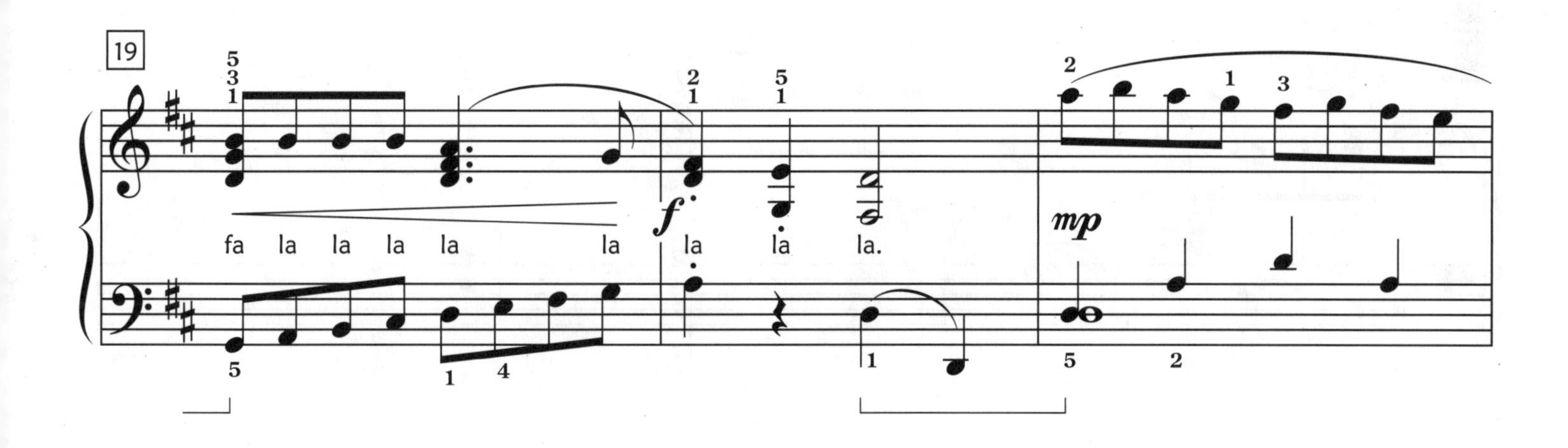
19
fa la la la la la la la la.
f
mp

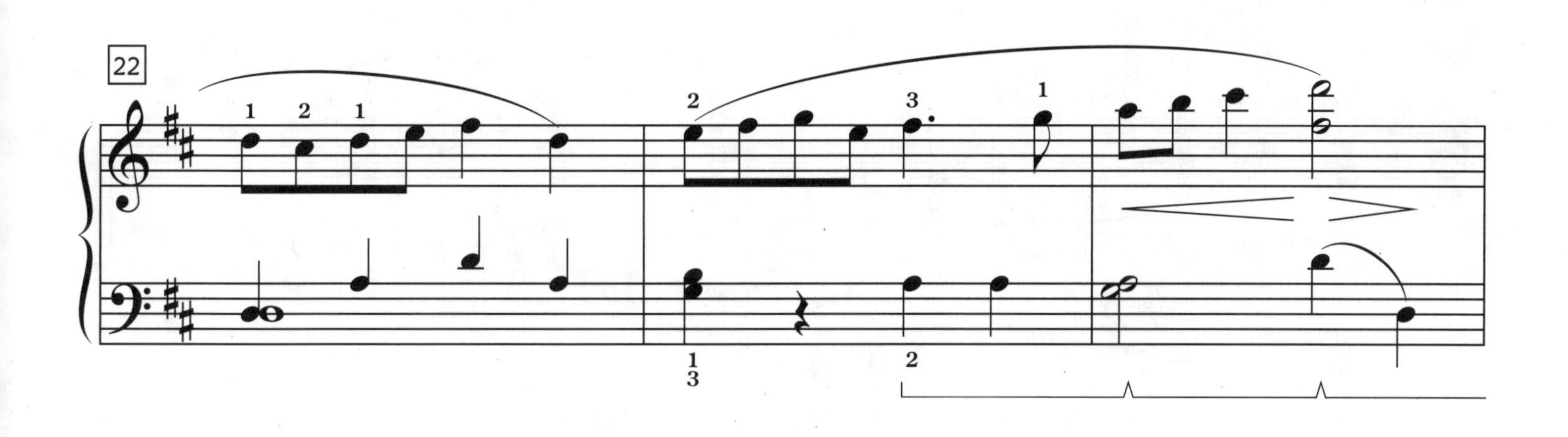
22

25

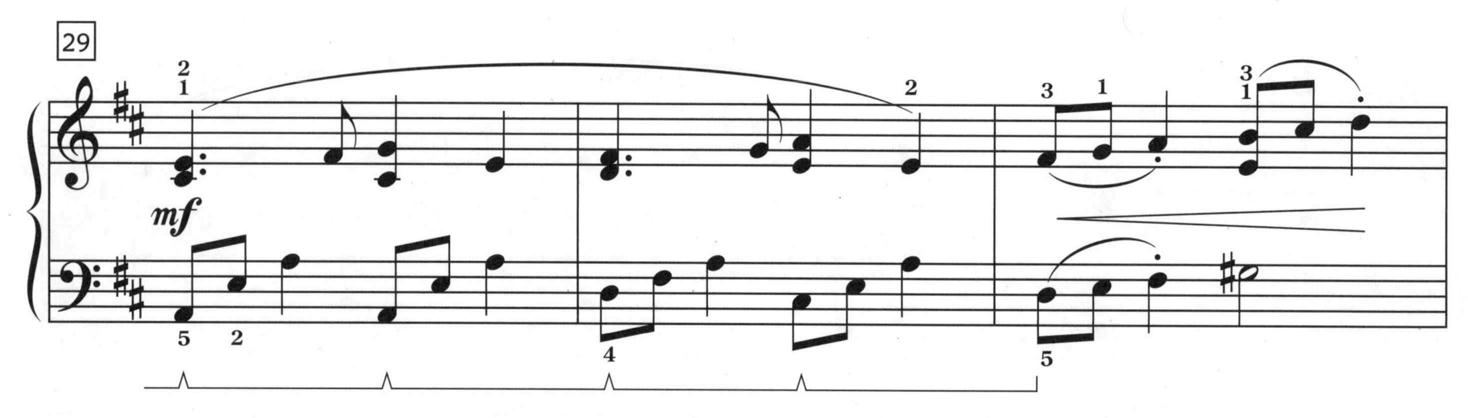
29
mf

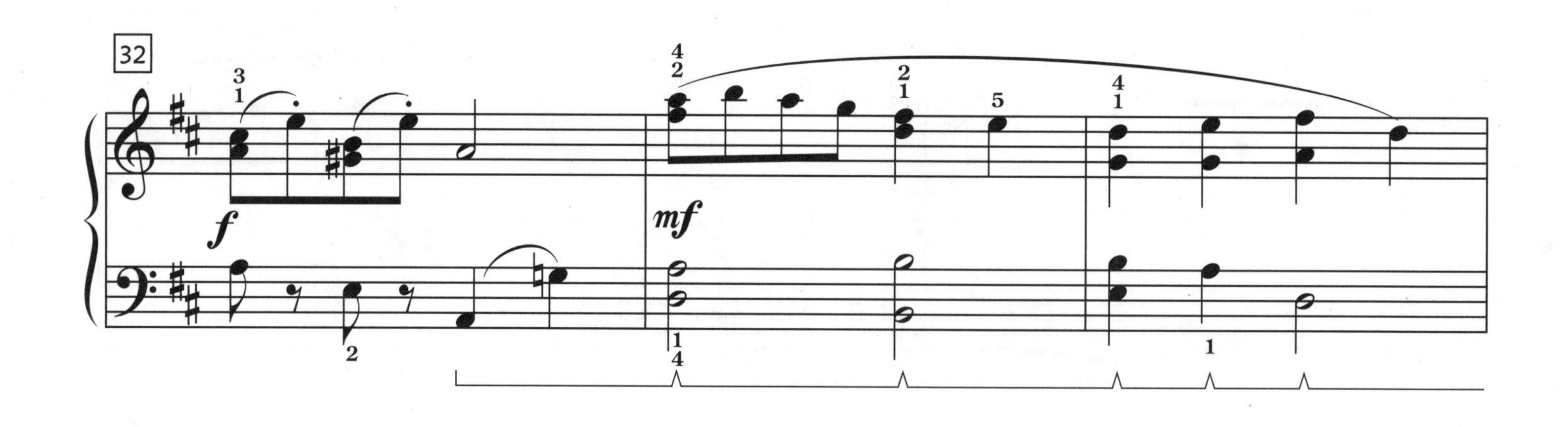
32
f
mf

35
f
mp

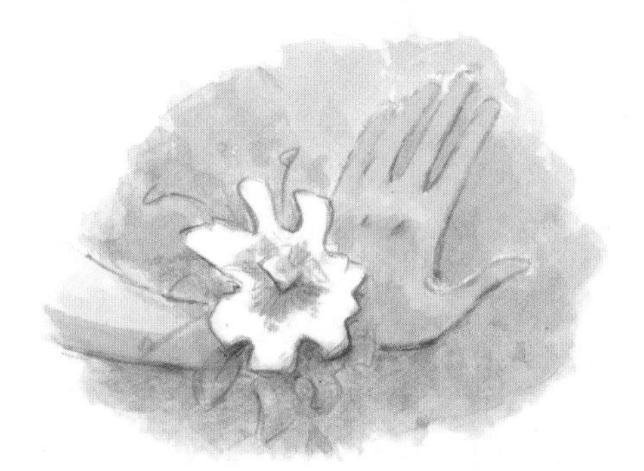

Waltz of the Flowers
(from *The Nutcracker*)

The premiere performance of Tchaikovsky's The Nutcracker *ballet in St. Petersburg in 1892 was not a success. But the music was so beautiful that Tchaikovsky selected eight of the more popular pieces and put them together to create* The Nutcracker Suite. ***Waltz of the Flowers*** *is one of the favorites from the suite. The flower dancers have a beautiful, graceful scene in Act Two of the ballet.*

Peter Ilyich Tchaikovsky

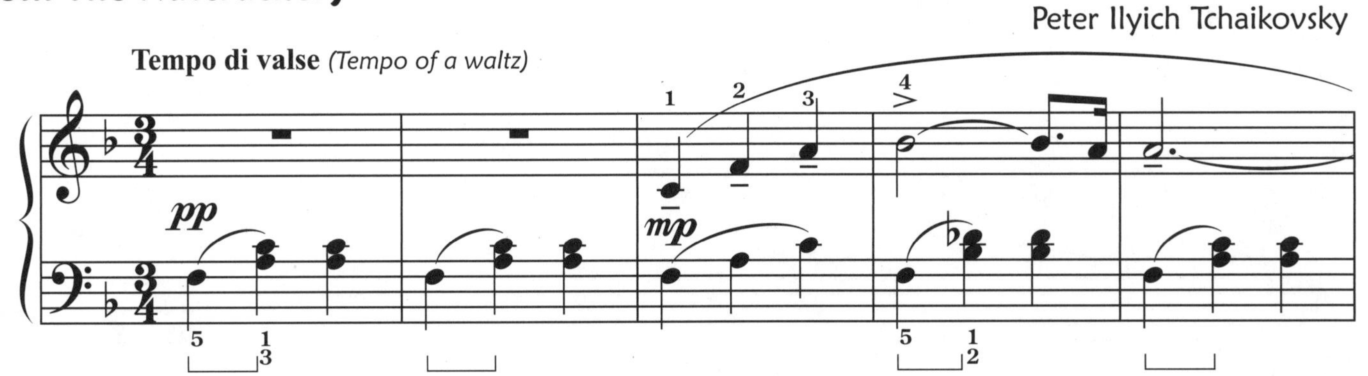

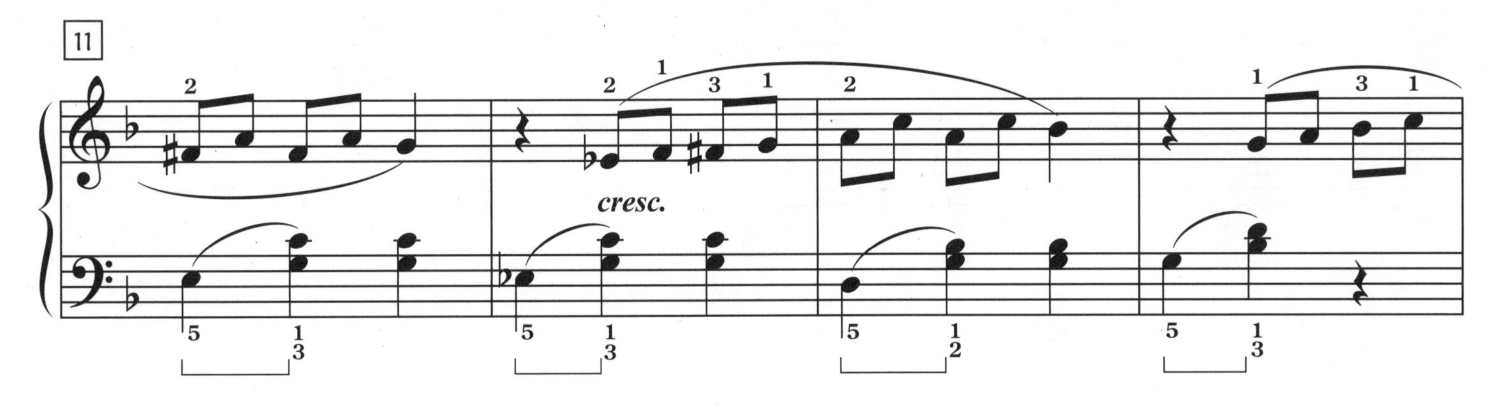

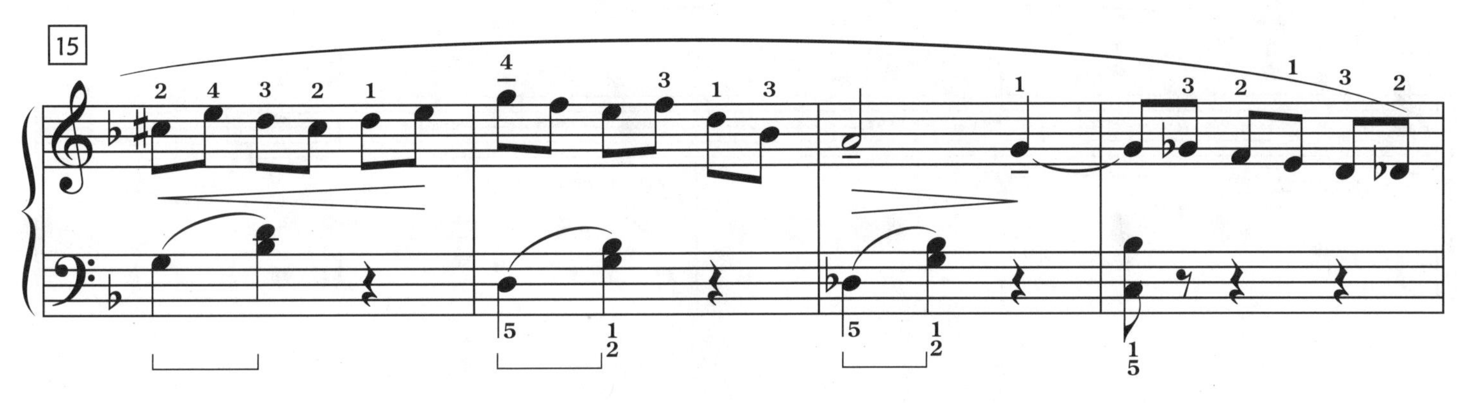

19
mp

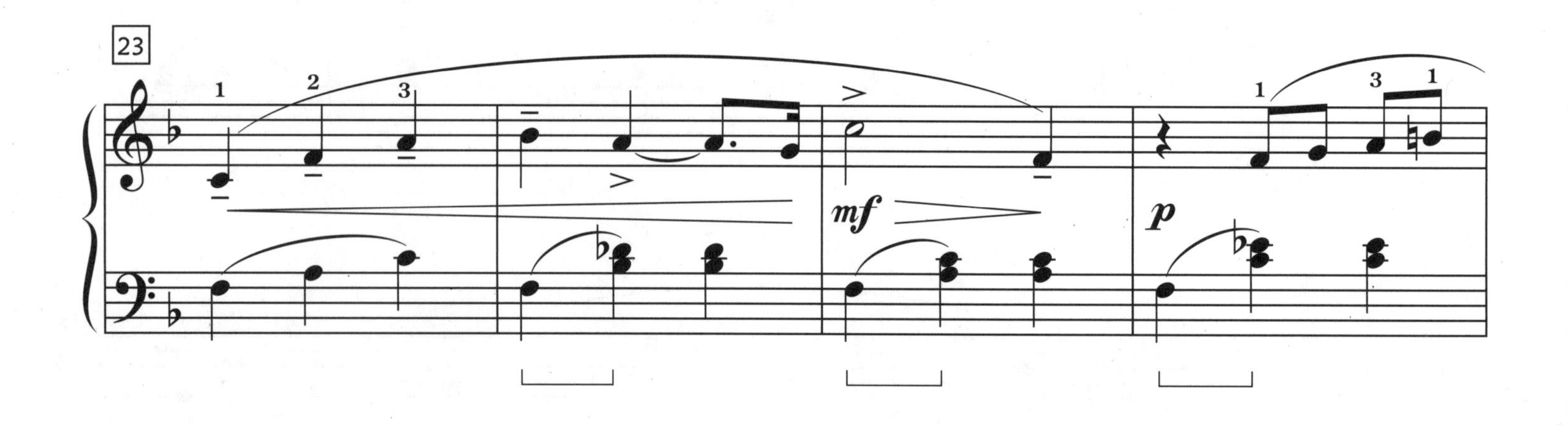
23
mf
p

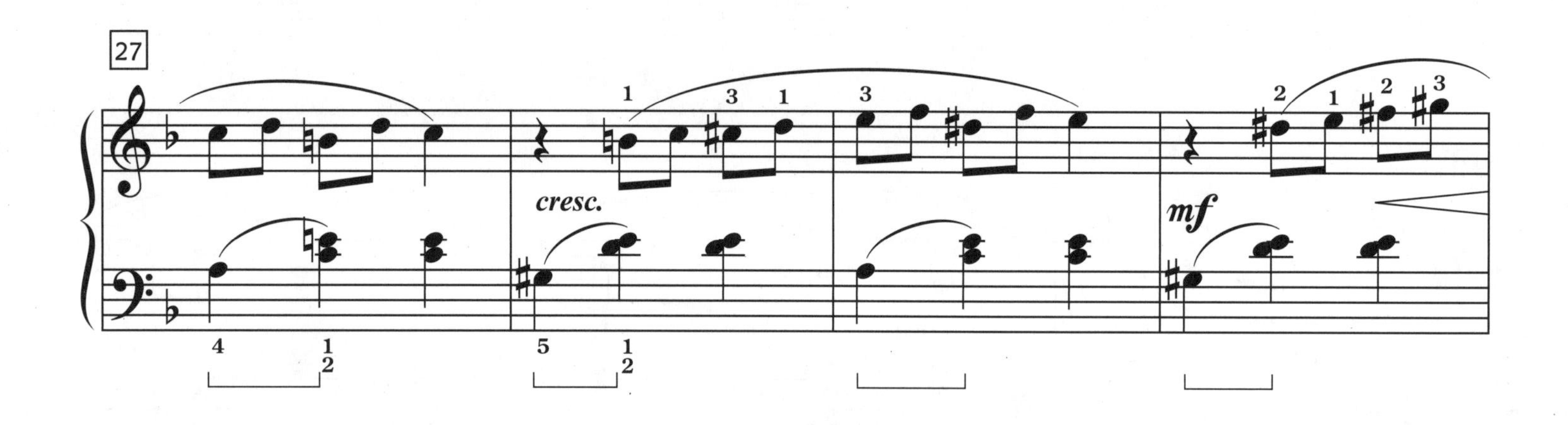
27
cresc.
mf

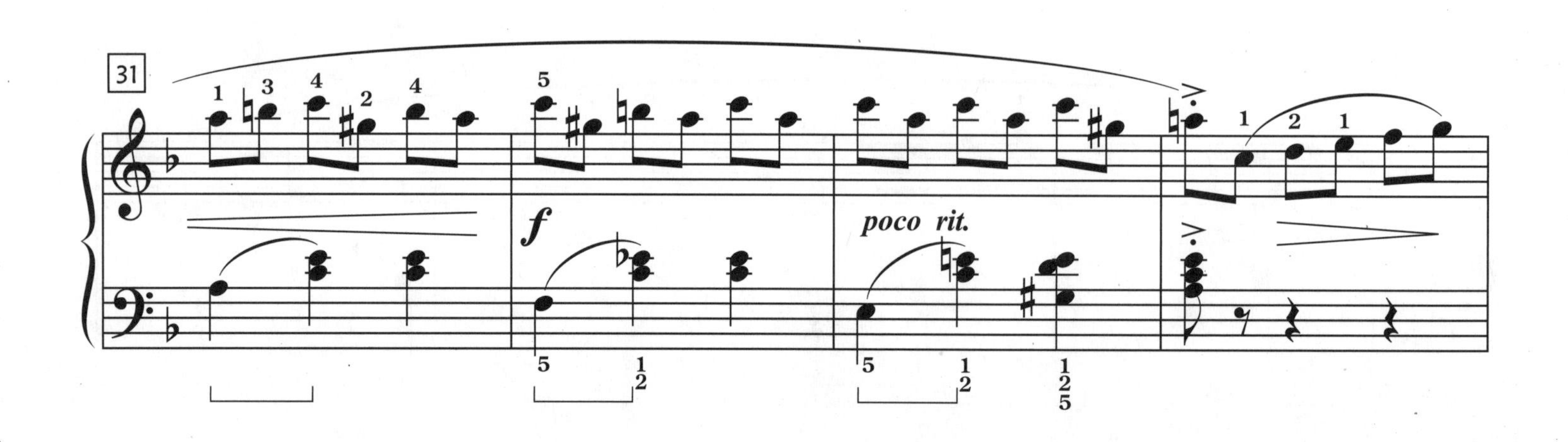
31
f
poco rit.

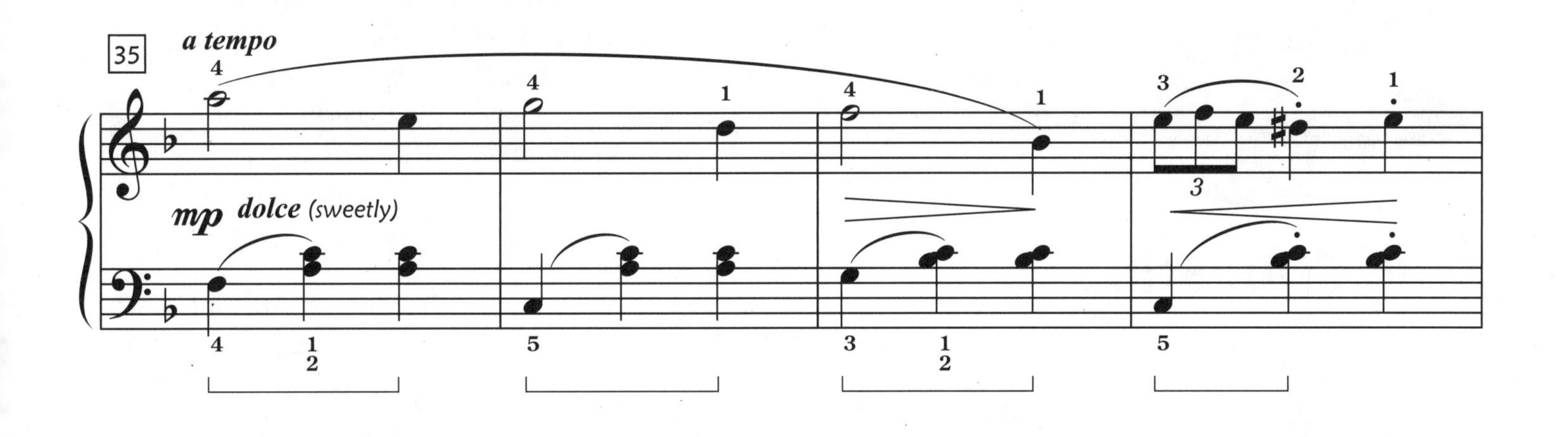

35
a tempo
mp dolce (sweetly)

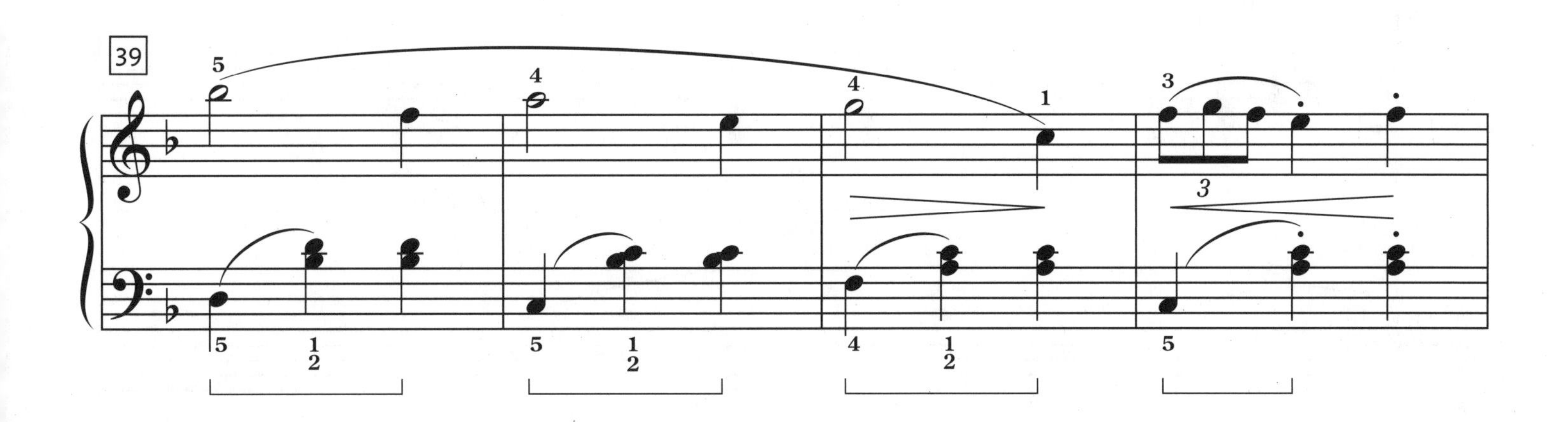

39

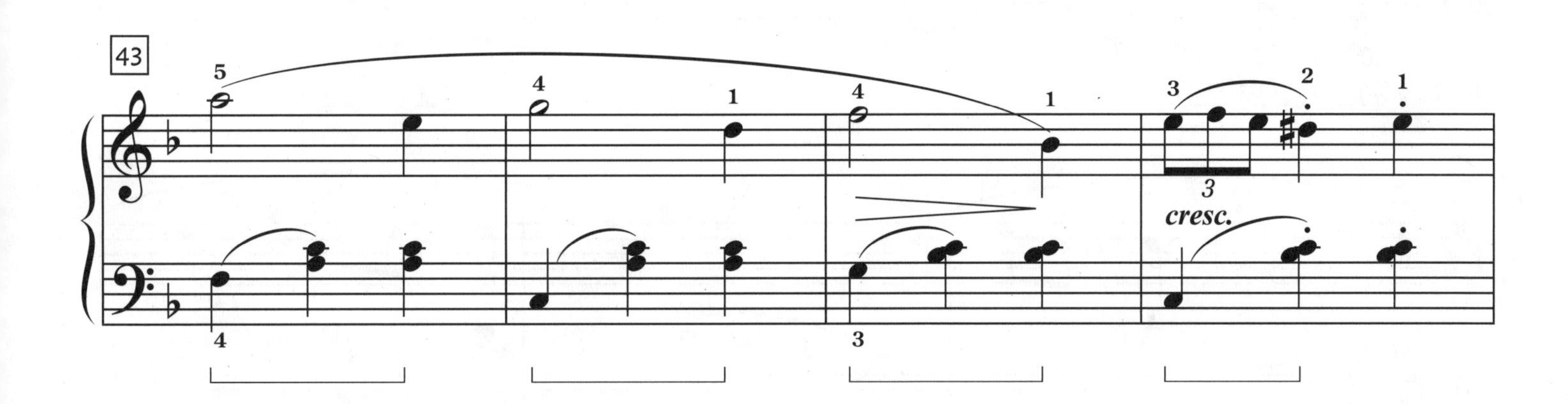

43
cresc.

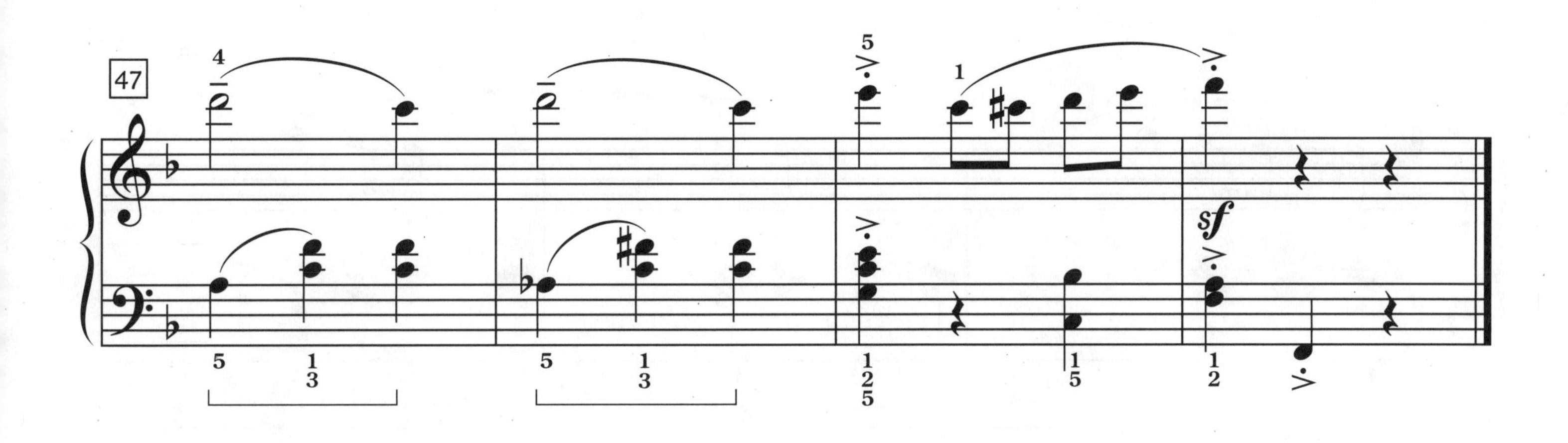

47
sf

Still, Still, Still *is a traditional Austrian Christmas song from the collection Salzburger Volkslieder (Salzburg Folk Songs) of 1819. The beautiful melody became particularly popular in the United States following the release of a version by the music group Mannheim Steamroller.*

Still, Still, Still

Traditional Austrian Carol

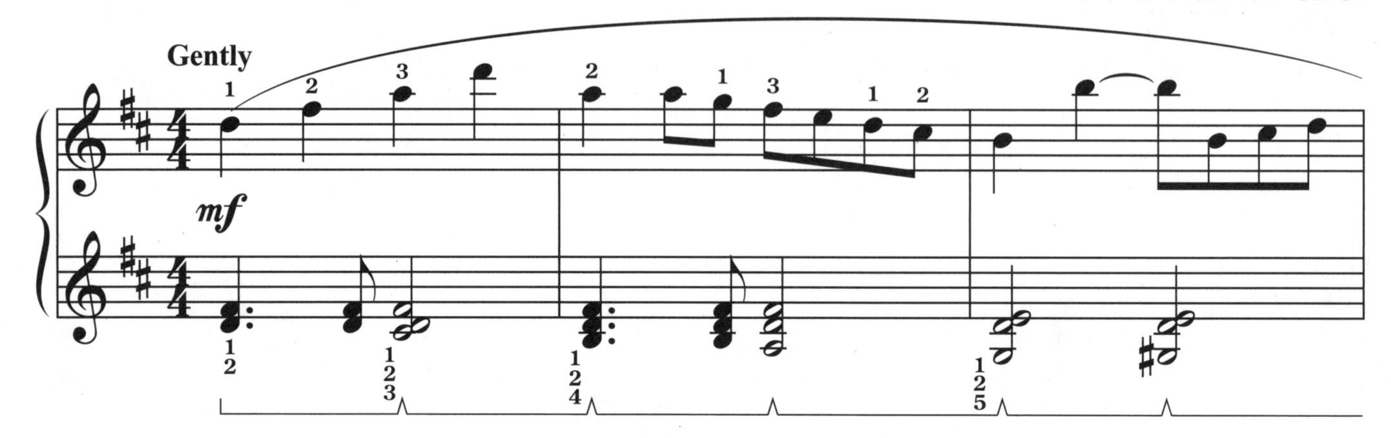

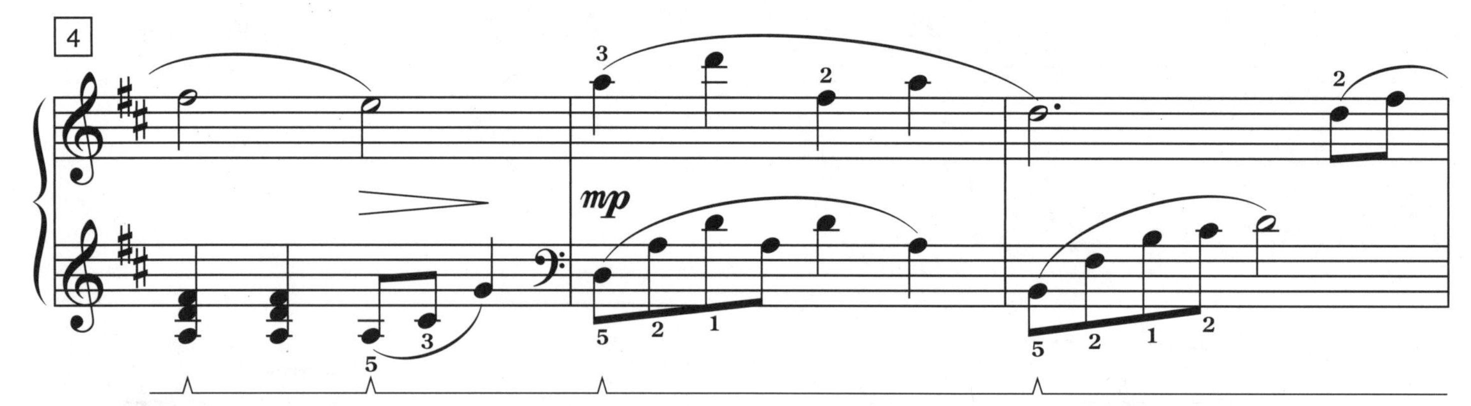

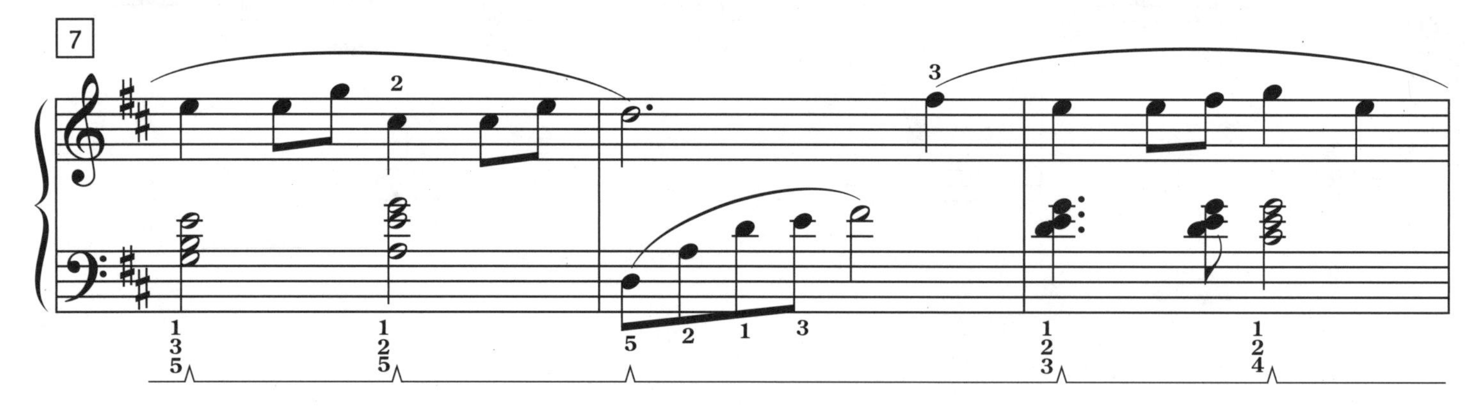

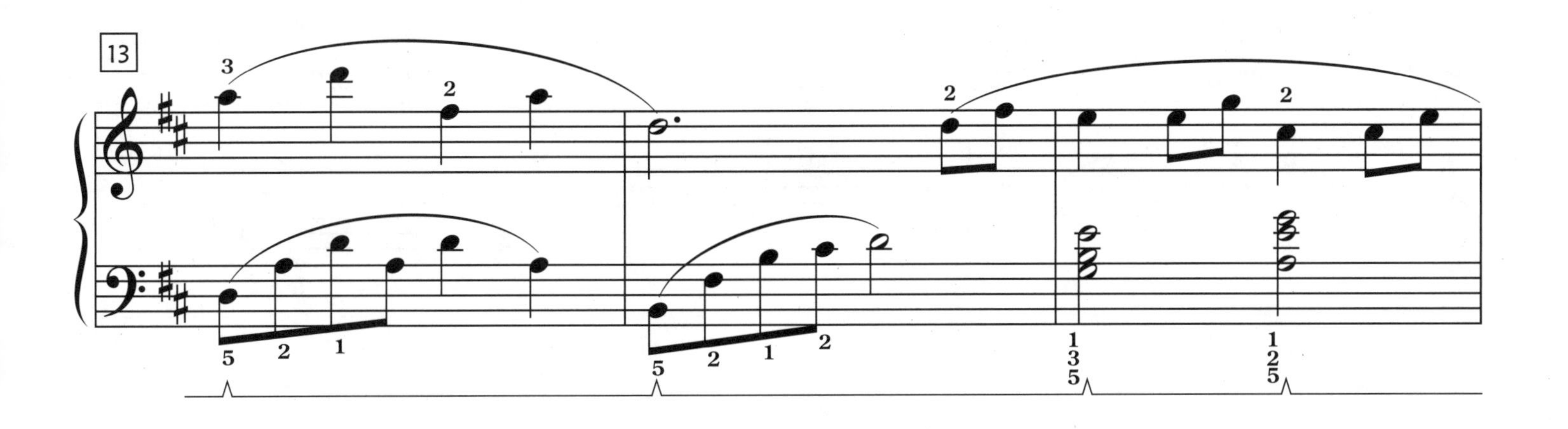
13

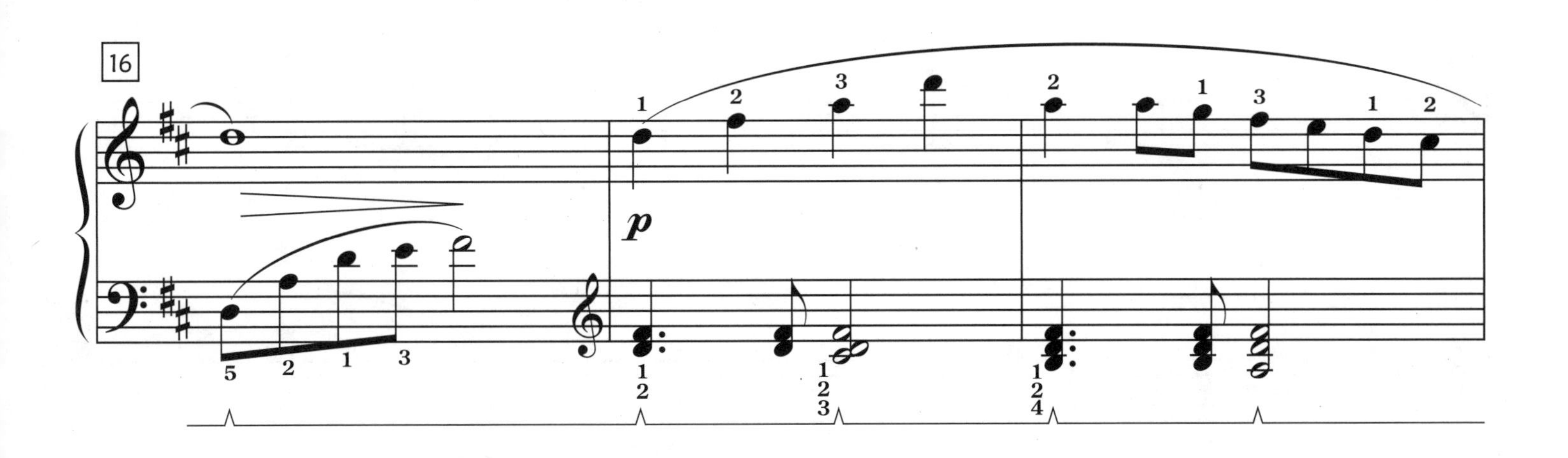
16
p

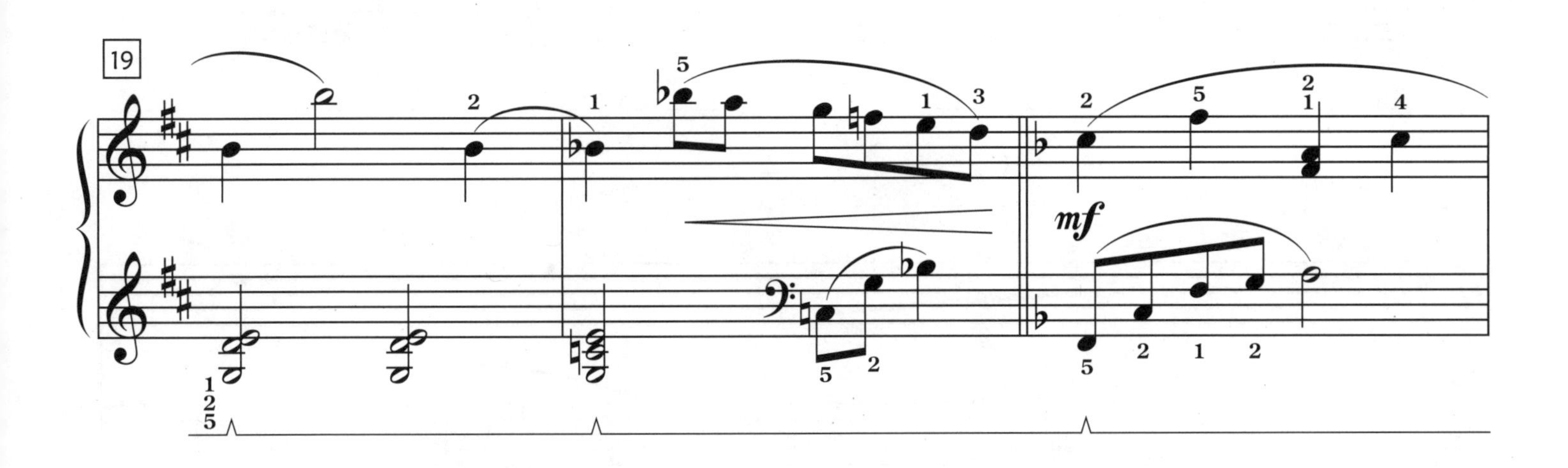
19
mf

22
mp

25
28
f
31
mp
34
36
p
poco rit.
8va